Behind Bars
The Hidden Architecture
of England's Prisons

Behind Bars
The Hidden Architecture
of England's Prisons

Allan Brodie

Jane Croom

James O Davies

First published 1999, by English Heritage at the
National Monuments Record Centre, Great Western
Village, Kemble Drive, Swindon SN2 2GZ.
Telephone: (44) (0)1793 414700
e-mail: info@rchme.gov.uk
World Wide Web: http://www.rchme.gov.uk

Published with the aid of HM Prison Service.

The Royal Commission on the Historical
Monuments of England and English Heritage
merged on 1st April 1999.

ISBN 1 873592 39 6

British Library Cataloguing in Publication Data

A CIP catalogue record for this book is available
from the British Library

Designed by Shawn Stipling,
Aquarium Graphic Design

Printed by HM Prison Service

Edited by Gillian Haggart

Graphics by Tony Berry

Additional research by Gary Winter

Photographs printed by Shaun Watts

Contents

Foreword

In my experience as a Governor few people can resist an offer of a visit to a prison. They exert a compelling fascination. This is probably because what happens inside them is beyond the experience of most people and their reality needs to be tested. There is also an element of fear and apprehension, since prisons represent a tangible horror: something that wrongdoers deserve, but something that could happen to us all, if our lives went badly wrong.

Many of our prisons are steeped in history and provide visual evidence of the kind of society which built them. While the outside face is often the most expressive and architecturally arresting, inside is a world which is closed except to those who live and work within it. Sometimes the outside and interior buildings are just as interesting and in almost every case the sense of history is just as evident. Invariably these internal buildings have been altered, usually because ideas about the purpose of imprisonment have changed or because of the need to house and occupy an increased number of prisoners. These changes have produced lots of modifications to the original buildings. Former condemned cells become offices, workshops are built on exercise yards, and cells designed to house one prisoner are rebuilt to hold two or more and to provide an 'en-suite' facility.

Many of the prisons in which I have served were not even purpose built. These have included a military camp and a stately home. These sorts of prisons have probably undergone most changes during this decade, as apart from a vastly increased prisoner population, huge sums have been spent recently on extra security defences to reduce escapes. Such prisons hold many surprises. One that I know of contains a superb Georgian dining room with a highly ornate suspended ceiling. My near-neighbour prison is an ex-RAF camp which displays a range of renovated artefacts to celebrate the prison's former use. Another boasts a superb panelled dance hall.

Almost all of our prisons have something else in common too. They are photogenic, often marvellously so. The authors of this book have recognised this and knew that a photographic record was required. They have managed to combine artistry, great skill and research to create an informative and vivid historical record. The Royal Commission on the Historical Monuments of England and the Prison Service are to be congratulated for supporting such an imaginative and worthwhile project.

D Waplington
Governor, HMP & YOI Moorland

Preface

Over the past three years a project team from the Royal Commission on the Historical Monuments of England (RCHME) has visited every working prison in England and Wales — as well as a number of former prisons. The survey's main aim was to record the current appearance of prisons and by combining this with detailed historical research produce a history of prison architecture (which will be the subject of a much larger book to be published by the RCHME). But because history is also being made today, the survey has concentrated as much on today's developments as on events which happened in the 1790s.

Architecture is about buildings but it is also about people — those who live in it and those who work in it. A conscious part of the survey has been to record aspects of life in modern prisons, partly for posterity but also to make comparisons with prison life for previous generations. The Prison Service has afforded us a unique opportunity to record England's prisons. We have been granted permission to go anywhere, photograph almost anything — except where this could compromise security — and speak to anyone. Everyone featured in this book has agreed to be photographed and we are very grateful for their help and patience.

This book explains briefly how prison buildings and conditions have changed during the last 250 years. It also includes a wide selection of images, past and present, which describe the main elements of a prison and the activities which take place in them. We hope it will be widely available to anyone living and working in today's prisons who has shown an interest in our work. We also hope that it will reach a wider public, including those who only know prisons through newspaper headlines and TV dramas, and lastly, that it will contribute to an appreciation of our prisons.

Behind Bars
The Evolution of English
Prison Architecture

Prisons before Howard

Until the late 18th century, most offenders were punished by execution, corporal punishment, transportation or fines. Prisons were mostly used to house people before their trial or until their punishment was carried out, although financial crimes including debt had been punished by a prison sentence since the 14th century. Prison was also used to enforce the laws passed by the Church, the Universities at Oxford and Cambridge, and the stannary courts of the tin mining districts in Devon and Cornwall. It was also used to punish breaches of forest law, and the large tower at Lydford (Devon) was probably used to hold these prisoners and those who breached the stannary laws.

Prisons had to be located in secure buildings, and until the 18th century this often meant using space within existing buildings. Usually part of the county town castle was employed as the county gaol. HMP Lancaster still occupies an existing castle, and when new wings were added during the 18th and 19th centuries the architects designed them to blend with the earlier buildings. In towns, prisons were located in the town gates, on bridges or in civic buildings. They were also located in buildings which were essentially indistinguishable from adjacent houses and this practice continued until the late 18th century.

During the 18th century, new prisons became larger. In the 1770s the Corporation at Bath built a new prison in a similar style to that used in the large Georgian townhouses being erected in Bath at the time. At the other end of the country, the Westmorland County Gaol was also being rebuilt on a new site in

top: Lydford Castle, Devon. General view of tower (late 12th and 13th centuries), used to hold prisoners in breach of forest and stannary laws.

bottom: Former prison, Bath. General view of street elevation (1770–3). Thomas Warr Atwood. The symmetrical façade with rusticated ground floor and pedimented windows mirror contemporary Georgian buildings still seen in the streets of Bath.

right: HMP Lancaster, Lancashire. One of the wings added by architect Thomas Harrison in 1793, built in a 'medieval style'.

left: Wheatley, Oxfordshire. General view of the small pyramid-shaped lock-up, built in 1834 by Mr Cooper.

top right: Bradford-on-Avon, Wiltshire. The highly decorative, 'pepper-pot' lock-up on the bridge (17th century). To prevent escape through the roof, some lock-ups were built with elaborate stone ceilings.

bottom right: Late 19th-century photograph of Newgate prison, London (demolished). Built by George Dance, junior (1770–83). Ventilation and light were restricted due to the absence of any openings on the street elevations of the buildings. The site is now occupied by the Old Bailey.

Appleby. Like the prison at Bath, Appleby is built in a style comparable to local domestic buildings, but in keeping with the local domestic style of Westmorland resembles a small, two-storied, double-pile house.

Lock-ups

The most common type of prison erected in the 17th and 18th centuries was the 'lock-up' — a small secure building to detain disorderly individuals for short periods. Typically lock-ups comprised a single room, and, although they were often simple secure square blocks constructed of readily-available local building materials, some were treated as lavish features in the heart of a village. At Wheatley there is a small pyramid-shaped lock-up, while at Lingfield the structure known locally as 'the cage' was built in 1773 adjacent to the 15th century cross and the village pond.

To prevent escape through the roof, some lock-ups were built with elaborate stone domes and this often resulted in a highly decorative, pepper-pot appearance, as at Bradford-on-Avon.

Newgate (1770–1783)

The final and grandest prison erected prior to the full impact of late 18th-century penal reform was Newgate. In 1755 the City of London had decided to rebuild the prison which was still located in the medieval gatehouse, but this scheme was dropped due to a lack of funds. It was revived in 1767 when George Dance, Senior, was appointed as the Surveyor, but due to his ill health his son took over in February 1769. The foundation stone of the new prison was laid on the 31 May 1770 and the whole prison was completed in 1780. However, on 6 June 1780 the Gordon rioters attacked the prison to liberate

captured comrades, resulting in serious damage. Repairs were completed by 1783, when public executions were transferred from Tyburn to Newgate.

Although Newgate was a monumental architectural presence in the City of London, its plan was very old-fashioned in terms of penal reform. John Howard, in commenting on Newgate said that, 'Many inconveniences of the old Gaol are avoided in this new one: but it has some manifest errors'. Although inmates were broadly separated by sex and age, the plan of the prison allowed only limited segregation. Ventilation and light were restricted due to the absence of any openings on the exterior of the buildings, and they were further inhibited by the buildings being grouped around three courtyards. Newgate's demolition began in 1902, and its site is now occupied by the Central Criminal Court (the Old Bailey).

John Howard (1773–1790)

John Howard (1726–90) was appointed as the High Sheriff of Bedfordshire in 1773 and as sheriff was responsible for the management of the county gaol. He discovered that prisoners were detained after being found innocent or after completing their sentence because they had not paid a discharge fee. He therefore applied to the justices to abolish fees and appoint a salaried gaoler. They insisted on Howard providing a precedent for this, and, in search of one, he began by visiting neighbouring counties where he discovered, 'scenes of calamity, which I grew daily more and more anxious to alleviate'.

In March 1774, when Howard attended the House of Commons to give evidence about prison conditions, he had already visited a large part of England. His evidence led to two Acts of Parliament being passed which abolished discharge fees and attempted to improve the health of prisoners.

Although Howard could have ceased his investigations at that stage, having achieved his immediate goal, he nevertheless continued his investigations, travelling throughout England and Ireland until March 1775, when he made his first visit to European prisons. In total he made seven journeys around Europe reaching as far as Moscow, Constantinople, Lisbon and Malta. In between the longer of these trips he continued to visit British prisons. The result of these journeys was his book: *The State of the Prisons*, published in 1777, with revised and enlarged editions appearing in 1780, 1784 and 1791.

Howard's last journey began in July 1789, a week before the Storming of the Bastille — a prison which he had visited a few years before. He travelled along the Baltic coast to St Petersburg and Moscow. He died in January 1790 in southern Russia of typhus, ironically of the same disease he had proved resistant to throughout his hundreds of visits to prisons.

'The State of the Prisons' — pits, vermin and disease

The buildings which Howard saw on his travels were rarely purpose-built and were usually in a poor state of repair. Even purpose-built, modern prisons, such as St George's Fields in Surrey (built in 1772), had dirty rooms where chickens roamed. Many prisons had no sewers or water supply, and urban prisons with cramped sites often had no exercise yards. Inmates were sometimes detained in subterranean pits and many were forced to sleep directly on the ground. Vermin were a problem in some prisons. At Knaresborough an officer who had been imprisoned for a few days, '... took in with him a dog to defend him from vermin; but the dog was soon destroyed, and the Prisoner's face was much disfigured by them'.

Howard noted that disease and filth were brought into prisons by new inmates as well as arising because of conditions within them. He recognised that 'Many who went in healthy, are in a few months changed to emaciated dejected objects'.

The diet of inmates was dependent on their ability to pay fees, so for poor inmates a period in prison could mean death. Poor prisoners relied on alms or charitable legacies, but inmates with money could enjoy a comfortable lifestyle, including the right to be released during the day.

Bust (by John Bacon) of John Howard on the gate of HMP Shrewsbury. John Hiram Haycock (1787–93).

General view of Littledean Gaol, Gloucestershire, built in the late 1780s by William Blackburn. The most complete surviving prison of the period.

Howard's ideal prison

John Howard systematically documented the conditions in England's prisons for the first time and provided incontrovertible evidence to show why reforms were necessary. He put forward proposals for improving conditions, and produced a design for an ideal prison. He advocated that the gaoler should be a good and sober man who lived in the prison and was constantly at home. He recommended that, like the gaoler, the chaplain and surgeon should be paid a salary, as all fees would be abolished.

Howard's ideal prison building was to consist of a series of square or rectangular blocks containing separate accommodation for male and female felons, male and female debtors and young criminals. At the heart of the prison would be the gaoler's house, with an infirmary and chapel at the rear of the site. Most of the blocks would have vaulted, open arcades on the ground floor, which could serve as an exercise area in wet weather and improve the circulation of air. Each inmate was to have his or her own sleeping cell located on the upper floors.

The National Penitentiary

An 18th century alternative to prison was transportation to America (as well as the stocks, pillory, corporal punishment and fines). Transportation to America ceased with the outbreak of hostilities in 1775 (the American War of Independence). This was expected to be a temporary interruption. An Act was passed in 1776 which initially authorised using hulks (former ships) for housing inmates for two years.

By 1778 with the declaration of independence by the USA, it was clear that transportation to America would not resume. In August 1786, however, the Government finally decided to use Botany Bay, and the first convict transports duly arrived in Australia on January 26 1788. In the next 80 years around 150,000 prisoners were sent there.

Meanwhile, an Act of Parliament was passed in 1779 to create a pair of penitentiaries for 600 men and 300 women. Prisoners were to sleep in heated single cells and were all to receive a standard diet. During the day inmates were expected to carry out work '...of the hardest and most servile Kind, in which Drudgery is chiefly required...'.

A £100 prize awarded by the government was won in 1782 by William Blackburn who designed the male prison; Thomas Hardwick won £60 for his design for the female prison. The cost of the male prison was estimated as £149,982, and the female prison, £60,370. The Treasury was reluctant to fund this and after prolonged negotiations the scheme was dropped. However, the 1779 Penitentiary Act did have a profound effect on the future development of prisons. It established a regime based on separate sleeping cells with limited association during the day, the associated or congregate system, the system employed in most prisons until the 1840s. It also introduced William Blackburn as the leading exponent of penal architecture.

William Blackburn and 1780s prisons

Although prolific, relatively little of the work of William Blackburn (1750–1790) survives. Survivals include the gate at HMP Dorchester, and the former gate at HMP Gloucester (see below; now flanked by two Victorian wings) — but the most substantial remnant within a working prison is the present administration building of HMP Stafford. A number of Blackburn's buildings also survive at Oxford Castle (a working prison until 1996), and a nursing home at Horsley in Gloucestershire retains features from the bridewell. The combined keeper's house and gate at Northleach is now a museum. Perhaps the most striking survival, however, is the picturesque bridewell at Littledean.

Blackburn was not the only architect working in the 1780s, although his work accounted for almost half of the prisons built during that decade. In Norfolk there are two surviving prisons from this period by unknown architects. Wymondham Bridewell was built between 1783 and 1785. It consisted of a large front block containing a committee room, a matron's room and accommodation for the keeper, with two narrow wings containing twenty-one cells behind it. The rear range of the former house of correction at Little Walsingham has four cells opening off the corridor on each of the two floors, and there are two large rooms which were probably originally a dayroom and a chapel or infirmary.

right: Walsingham House of Correction, Norfolk (1787). Four cells open off the corridor on each of the two floors.

below: Three-dimensional reconstruction of William Blackburn's 1780s prison, HMP Gloucester, Gloucestershire. The original gate at Gloucester is the only building to survive, sandwiched between two later wings.

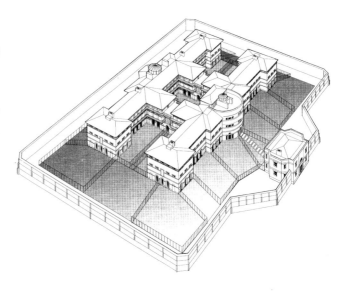

The Next Generation of Prisons

In the early 1790s a number of changes occurred which affected the construction of prisons. The counties that had decided to rebuild their county gaols or houses of correction were near to completing their building programmes — although some cities, towns and boroughs continued to rebuild their existing prisons. The resumption of transportation removed some of the pressure for new large national penitentiaries and large county gaols.

The spiritual and architectural leaders of the reformed prison architecture, Howard and Blackburn, both died in 1790 and the outbreak of war with France in 1793 probably helped to deter new construction schemes. There was to be no new nationwide building campaign for prisons on the scale of the late 1780s for over fifty years until the completion of Pentonville in 1842.

At the beginning of the 19th century, a few counties which had not previously reformed their prisons began a reconstruction programme, and there was also a need for prisoner of war camps.

Byfield and Alexander

Two architects were responsible for the most important projects of this period, George Byfield (c 1756–1813) and Daniel Asher Alexander (1768–1846). In four related designs, Byfield developed a plan which was to become the most popular form of county gaol and town prison during the early 19th century. A central block usually contained accommodation for the governor and a committee room on the ground floor, while on the first floor there was a chapel for the inmates. It might also contain infir-

maries on the top storey. This block was surrounded by separate wings which were linked at the first floor level to the chapel by iron walkways.

The most monumental example of this plan was Alexander's County Gaol at Maidstone (now HMP Maidstone). Around a tall central circular building there were three cruciform complexes of wings, each with a smaller circular block at its heart. One of the three groups of wings and the governor's house survive.

left: Crescent wing, HMP Stafford, Staffordshire (1834 with 1864 additions). Originally built with a group of treadwheels in front of its curved façade. Treadwheels became such important features in some prisons that other buildings were arranged around them.

top right: HMP Maidstone, Kent (1810–23). Governor's house, built by Daniel Asher Alexander (1768–1846).

bottom right: HMP Maidstone, Kent. Block plan showing the present layout of the prison buildings. Three cruciform complexes of wings, each with a smaller circular block at its heart, surrounded the tall central circular building.

Prisoner of war camps

Alexander was also responsible for the prisoner of war camp at Dartmoor, one of the prisons built to hold French prisoners of war. The earliest was at Norman Cross (Cambridgeshire) of which little survives, but parts of the original prisons at Dartmoor and Perth survive within the current ones. Both were different from contemporary prisons because of the regime under which prisoners of war were detained. There was no need to separate them into categories, and to hold the largest numbers possible the blocks contained dormitories rather than cells. Dartmoor closed in 1816 and lay unused until 1850. Perth closed in 1814 and re-opened as Scotland's general prison in 1843.

Millbank (1812–1821)

Although the idea of a national prison had been first proposed in the 1770s, it was only with the need to provide accommodation for prisoners of war that government-funded prisons were built. The National Penitentiary was revived in 1810 and two years later work began on the construction of Millbank (demolished; the Tate Gallery now occupies the site).

During the 1790s Jeremy Bentham had advocated erecting his 'Panopticon' as the Penitentiary, but his design was never executed. Millbank, though executed, was an equally bizarre and impractical prison. Six pentagonal complexes of cell blocks radiated from a central hexagon in a design which can only be described as reminiscent of a snowflake. It was too complicated in layout, was badly built and was the most expensive prison erected in the period. It was also difficult to patrol and its complicated plan reputedly led to staff becoming lost. With all its problems, it is surprising that it continued to be used until the 1880s.

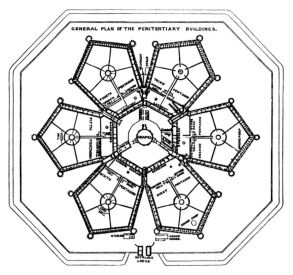

Millbank Penitentiary, London 1812–1821. Plan from Henry Mayhew and John Binny, The *Criminal Prisons of London and Scenes of Prison Life* 1862.

HMP Dartmoor, Devon. General view of site. The buildings at Dartmoor date from 1806–09, 1812, the late 19th, and early 20th centuries. The earliest buildings, built by Daniel Asher Alexander, were to accommodate French prisoners of war.

The 1823 Gaol Act and the treadwheel

Rather than embark on constructing further national prisons, the government preferred to enforce uniform practices in major prisons through the vehicle of the 1823 Gaol Act. Under that Act, justices of the peace were made responsible for the appointment of staff and for the state of the buildings. They had to ensure that inmates were held in separate classes according to their sex, age and crime and were required to enforce hard labour, normally through the use of the newly invented treadwheel.

Human-powered wheels had been in use for centuries, but in these the people had walked on the inside of a large-diameter wheel. In 1818 William Cubitt invented a wheel in which prisoners walked around the outer circumference, as if walking round a waterwheel (see page 79). This was rapidly adopted in dozens of prisons. Treadwheels became such important features in some prisons that other buildings were arranged around them. The house of correction at Brixton (now HMP Brixton), was partly polygonal in plan, with the tread-wheels in the centre overlooked by the governor's house. The crescent wing at HMP Stafford was built with a group of treadwheels in front of its curved face. Treadwheels ceased to be used in English prisons after the 1898 Prison Act, but many treadwheel houses survive in current prisons as workshops or stores.

A New Kind of Prison — the 'Separate System'

A major feature of the 1823 Gaol Act was the enforcement of an elaborate system of inmate classification. By the 1830s the original system separating males, females and juveniles (and within those categories further separating debtors, felons and misdemeanants) — had proliferated subdivisions, so that a prison such as Maidstone was expected to house twenty-nine separate categories of inmate.

Many prisons by then were up to fifty years old, and the only contemporary proposals for new prisons were simply enlarged versions of the plan developed by Byfield in circa 1800.

In a search for a way forward, the government turned for inspiration to recent prisons erected in the USA. William Crawford (1788–1847) visited America, where two systems of discipline had developed. He observed how under the 'silent system' of Auburn and Sing-Sing prisons, prisoners worked together but slept in individual cells, passing their lives in total silence; and how, under the 'separate system' at Eastern State Penitentiary in Philadelphia, inmates were held in solitary confinement, occupying their cells day and night. Crawford favoured the latter system and, together with Reverend Whitworth Russell (d.1847) and Joshua Jebb (1793–1863), devised plans for prisons in which to implement it.

Pentonville (1840–1842)

The separate system was first enforced at Pentonville, a model penitentiary for 520 convicts, erected in 1840–2. Selected adult males, who were first-offenders sentenced to less than fifteen years, spent the first eighteen months of their sentence in separate confinement at Pentonville, working alone in their cells. Their conduct at Pentonville determined their status when they arrived in the Antipodes. Parkhurst, which had opened in 1838, fulfilled a similar role for juveniles.

Although Pentonville was a convict prison, it became the model for the redevelopment of local prisons. It had a radial layout with four cell blocks around a central hall. The wings had three stories with cells on either side of a central open corridor, the upper tiers of cells being reached from galleries. This arrangement allowed staff on the ground floor to see all the levels in the wing, and each wing could also be observed from the centre of the prison. The staff in turn were supervised by the governor and the prison's commissioners who had offices adjacent to the centre.

The cells measured 13' by 7' by 10' high (3.9m x 2.1m x 2.7m), and were designed to prevent communication between prisoners. They contained all the necessities of prison life, including a hammock, table, water closet, basin and gas light. The prisoners ate, slept and worked in their cells, leaving them only for religious worship and exercise. The cell windows could not be opened and therefore a heating and ventilation system had to be included (see page 62).

The strict segregation extended to both the exercise yards and the chapel. Individual, wedge-shaped yards were arranged in circular groups around a central observation post. These were later replaced by exercise rings (see page 94), around which lines of inmates walked in crocodile fashion. In the chapel each inmate had their own individual pew which allowed them to see the

preaching clergyman but prevented contact with other inmates.

By 1850 around sixty British prisons had been rebuilt or were being altered to conform to the separate system — a building campaign which provided about 11,000 separate cells. Between 1842 and 1877, nineteen radial prisons were erected in England. They generally had 200 to 400 cells, although those serving large urban areas sometimes held between 500 and 1000 inmates. Most of the accommodation was for adult males, but women had their own cell block and some prisons also had wings for juveniles and debtors. Pentonville-style wings were also added to some existing prisons, and at others the existing buildings were altered or progressively rebuilt.

right: HMP Pentonville, London. William Crawford, Revd Whitworth Russell and Joshua Jebb (1840–2 and later additions). Block plan showing radial layout with four cell blocks around a central hall. Pentonville was the first prison in England and Wales in which the 'separate system' was implemented.

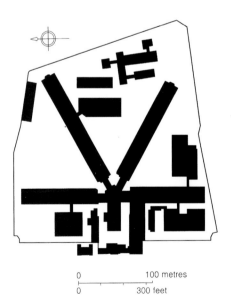

0   100 metres

0   300 feet

above: 'C' Wing, HMP Preston, Lancashire. Alfred Waterhouse (1860s). Like Pentonville, on a radial plan, although its four wings were built at different dates.

right: HMP Lewes, East Sussex, A Wing. Daniel Rowlinson Hill (1850–53).

left: HMP Manchester, Greater Manchester. Alfred Waterhouse (1864–8). Centre of the male prison.

above: HMP Leeds, West Yorkshire, centre of prison. Perkin and Backhouse (1843–7).

Convict Prisons

New prisons were needed after 1848 for convicts sentenced to work on public works prior to being transported, and further accommodation was required during the 1850s and 1860s when transportation ended (to be replaced by public works prisons).

Convicts — those prisoners who had been convicted of the most serious categories of crime — were initially confined either in hulks or in purpose-built prisons, like the one which opened at Portland in 1848, and at Portsmouth in 1852. The former prisoner of war prison at Dartmoor also reopened in 1850. The convicts worked in groups during the day and only occupied their cells at night. Their sleeping berths measured just 7' by 4' by 7' (2.1m x 1.2m x 2.1m) and were divided by corrugated iron partitions. One occupant of Portland described his cell as:

> ... nothing but a small corrugated iron kennel, with a stone or slate floor. There was not so much as a bit of wooden grating on the floor, so that a prisoner, when his boots and stockings were off, had to tread the icy-cold flags. The only articles of furniture in it were a wooden stool, a very diminutive flap table, and a hammock and bedding rolled up on a shelf or ledge in one corner.

During the 1850s sentences of penal servitude replaced transportation, which was finally abolished in 1867. New public works prisons also opened at Chatham (1856), Borstal (1874; now HMP Rochester), Chattenden (1877) and Dover (1884). In 1853 the government purchased the former house of correction at Brixton to hold female convicts, and after 1856, selected women

completed their sentence at Fulham Refuge, where they were trained in domestic skills to help them earn a living on their release. A new prison for females opened at Woking in 1869, adjacent to a prison for invalid male convicts which had opened in 1860.

Convict prisons began to close during the 1880s and 1890s, as fewer offenders received sentences of penal servitude and those who did were sentenced to shorter terms. Convicts were also able to spend their separate confinement in local prisons. Pentonville, Millbank and Wormwood Scrubs ceased holding convicts, and with insufficient numbers to justify large prisons for females and invalids, the establishments at Woking and Fulham closed.

below: Portland Convict Prison, Dorset. Late 19th-century photograph of a cell.

The Prison Commission and the Beginnings of the Borstal System

By 1877, over half the prisons which had been open just forty years earlier had closed. These were mainly small prisons which were unsuitable for the separate system. The closures continued under the 1877 Prison Act and by 1878 the number of prisons in England and Wales was further reduced from 113 to 69.

The 1877 Act also placed local prisons under the control of a central government body, the Prison Commission, whose first chairman was Edmund Du Cane. Du Cane had designed Wormwood Scrubs, which was erected as a convict prison between 1874 and 1891 (see page 22). Wormwood Scrubs had a telegraph-pole layout with four parallel cell blocks linked at their centre by covered walkways. The wings were orientated north–south to ensure that all cells received some sunlight during the day. In place of in-cell toilets and wash basins, they had projecting ablution towers.

Like Pentonville, Wormwood Scrubs was influential on local prison design and during the 1880s scaled-down versions of it were erected at Bristol, Nottingham, Norwich and Shrewsbury. These prisons had just two wings, male and female, the administration and chapel being attached to the men's wing. The cell blocks were linked to ancillary buildings by covered walkways.

Improvements were also made to local prisons including the removal of water closets from cells and their replacement by ablution towers. Anti-suicide measures such as raised gallery railings and wire netting

across open cell block corridors were introduced. Additional accommodation was created by converting basement stores into cells, by the heightening and lengthening of existing wings, and by the addition of new cell blocks. Ancillary buildings including new kitchens, laundries, receptions and hospitals, were erected at earlier prisons, removing these functions from the main body of the prison and destroying the simplicity of the radial plans.

In 1895 a committee chaired by Herbert Gladstone published its report on the administration of prisons and the treatment and classification of prisoners. Du Cane was replaced in the same year by Evelyn Ruggles-Brise, who implemented many of the Gladstone committee's recommendations. The Prison Commissioners were amalgamated with the Directors of Convict Prisons. The blocks of corrugated-iron sleeping berths at Portland and Dartmoor were replaced by wings containing solid cells. Unproductive labour was abolished. Instead prisoners were taught trades and worked together in cell-block corridors, in former treadwheel houses and in purpose-built workshops.

The *Gladstone Report* also led to the foundation of reformatories for inebriates, young offenders and habitual criminals. State Inebriate Reformatories were opened in 1900–01 at Warwick for 30 men, and at Aylesbury for 120 women. A reformatory for juvenile-adults (aged sixteen to twenty-one) was established in Borstal convict prison (now HMP Rochester, Kent) in 1902 — which was gradually rebuilt by the inmates after 1908.

Further borstal institutions were founded between 1906 and 1921 for

HMP Nottingham, Nottinghamshire. View of administration building/ chapel, with male wing behind. Alten Beamish (1889–91). Built on a model inspired by HMP Wormwood Scrubs.

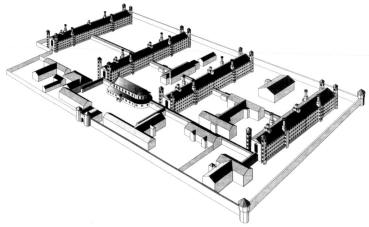

above: 'D' Wing, HMP Wormwood Scrubs, London. Edmund Du Cane (1874–91). The wings were orientated north–south to ensure that all cells received some sunlight during the day.

right: HMP Wormwood Scrubs, London. Three-dimensional reconstruction of original layout.

top: 'A' Wing, HMP Rochester, Kent (formerly Borstal Convict Prison; 1913).

bottom: Borstal, Kent (now HMP Rochester). Juvenile-adult prisoners building a cell block (c 1910).

boys at Lincoln, Feltham and Portland, and for girls at Aylesbury. Juvenile-adults spent between two and three years in a borstal institution where they were provided with education and training to help them make a living on their release. At Borstal in Kent, for instance, the young offenders undertook physical exercise, industrial training and agricultural work during the day and attended school lessons in the evening.

In 1912 a prison was opened at Camp Hill on the Isle of Wight for habitual criminals who had received an additional sentence of five to ten years preventive detention at the end of their sentence of penal servitude. It was located on a rural site and was designed to be less institutional than conventional prisons. A description of the newly opened prison at Camp Hill emphasised its pleasant surroundings:

> *What may be called a 'garden village' is being built, and as the site is on sloping ground in the forest, the grouping of the white, and red and white single, double and four cottage blocks amongst the trees, will give a most pleasing effect when completed.* (*Prison Commission Report 1913*, p 43)

The State Inebriate Reformatories never dealt with more than a minority of cases. Both had closed by 1918. Camp Hill was initially hailed as a great success in reforming adult recidivists, but by the 1920s it was recognised that many hardened criminals were incapable of change and the prison's main purpose became their removal from society. It ceased to be a preventive detention prison in 1935. The borstal system, however, went from strength to strength and continued to expand into the mid-20th century.

The Inter-War Years: Open Borstals and Open Prisons

On the eve of the First World War there were fifty-six local prisons, but by 1931 only twenty-seven were still open. The closures reflected a declining prison population, the daily average number of local prisoners having fallen to around 10,000. This allowed the development of open penal establishments, an idea inspired by Alexander Paterson who was appointed to the Prison Commission in 1922.

Paterson believed that prisons should not simply be cloakrooms or kennels, but should have a positive impact on an offender's behaviour. An inmate's personality should be developed by imprisonment through an active programme which included both physical and mental stimulation, as well as 'humanising and socialising influences'. To achieve this he first concentrated on developing the borstal system by introducing ideas from the public school system. In the long-term he hoped that prisons could be abolished and be replaced by specialised institutions for training and assessing prisoners.

In 1930 Major William W Llewellin led a group of boys from Feltham to Nottinghamshire to establish the first open borstal at Lowdham Grange, where he became its first governor. Lowdham Grange has now been rebuilt but much of the original open borstal remains at North Sea Camp, near Boston, which Major Llewellin also founded after a march from Stafford prison in May 1935. The boys lived in tents when they first arrived there while they built hutted accommodation behind the existing sea bank and reclaimed the marshes. Over 28 miles of dykes have been constructed and nearly 1000 acres of saltmarsh reclaimed for farmland. A third open borstal opened in 1938 at Hollesley Bay Colony.

In July 1931 Alexander Paterson proposed purchasing New Hall Wood so that adult inmates from Wakefield could work there, and by March 1934 it was decided that a camp should be established for that purpose. Initially a small camp was built to house fifty inmates during the week, but by March 1936 the site was officially declared a prison — New Hall Camp, the first open prison for adult prisoners.

HMP North Sea Camp, Lincolnshire (1935 ff). Founded by Major William W Llewellin, who led the borstal boys on a march from Stafford prison. The boys lived in tents, until they completed the building of this hutted accommodation behind the sea bank.

Post-War Years

The fall in the prison population ended during the Second World War, and since 1940 it has risen almost continuously. In 1940 the prison population was less than 10,000 but by 1950 it had more than doubled. The difficult economic circumstances after the War meant that new purpose-built prisons were unaffordable and so a number of former military sites were pressed into use. The Prison Commission took over a number of camps to use as open prisons and some are still in use. HMP Ford, which opened in 1960, was one of the last former camps to be adapted. Others, such as Leyhill, retain few of their original huts, most of the accommodation now being provided in modern purpose-built blocks.

The military had also taken over country houses during the War and a number of these became prisons. In 1946 Hewell Grange was sold to the Prison Commissioners for use as a borstal training centre. It is now an open prison for adult males who are accommodated in dormitories on the upper floors of the house.

Country houses were also acquired from other sources. Foston Hall is a red-brick, Jacobean style house, purchased from the Hardy family by Derbyshire County Council in 1947 who then sold it to the Prison Commission in 1954. It opened a year later as a junior detention centre for boys, and is now a prison. Like Hewell Grange some of the living accommodation is contained within the house.

At Kirklevington Grange, which opened in May 1963, most of the inmate accommodation is in blocks which were built during the 1970s adjacent to the house. The house, which is dated 1898, contains the administration and education facilities and some dormitories.

In addition to camps and country houses, the Prison Commission took over a number of children's homes for use as low-security institutions. In 1898 the Chorlton Board of Guardians established a cottage colony at Styal, so that children and babies could be held separately from the rest of the workhouse's inhabitants. It closed in 1956 and re-opened as a female prison in 1962. The blocks are arranged around a complex of streets and lawns, and the accommodation is designed to resemble large detached houses and pairs of semi-detached houses.

1930s huts of 'B' Wing, HMP Ford, West Sussex. The prison, which opened in 1960, was one of the last former military camps to be adapted for use as an open prison by the Prison Commission.

above: HMP Hewell Grange, Worcestershire. General view of the country house built by G F Bodley and T Garner (1884–91). It was sold to the Prison Commissioners in 1946 for use as a borstal training centre.

right: HMP Foston Hall, Derbyshire. General view of house built by Thomas Chambers Hine (1863). Sold to the Prison Commission in 1954, and opened in 1955.

Everthorpe and 'New Wave' Designs

Adapting former military sites and orphanages was an adequate short-term solution for low security prisons, but the Prison Commission also recognised the need for new purpose-built establishments. In the 1950 *Annual Report of the Prison Commission*, a plan was published for a secure prison holding 300 men and, although the site was unnamed, it is clear that it is an early draft of the scheme for HMP Everthorpe, which was built in 1956–8.

The inmate accommodation at Everthorpe consisted of two long wings each divided into two parts holding seventy-five inmates. The blocks have three stories of cells opening from landings flanking an open corridor which was top-lit by glass bricks set into the concrete, barrel-vaulted ceiling. The wings were linked to a central amenities complex by a single-storied secure corridor, with a separate industrial area at the rear of the site. Everthorpe was essentially only a development of the ideas first employed at Wormwood Scrubs.

The 1959 White Paper *Penal Practice in a Changing Society* stated that '... the present buildings stand as a monumental denial of the principles to which we are committed'.

Nevertheless, before a new type of prison could be developed, some of the schemes mooted in the late 1940s and early 1950s were already in progress.

Plans for the psychiatric hospital at Grendon had been drawn up by 1956. Like Everthorpe, the wings were to have the cells flanking an open corridor, and the male holding block

was to have a Y-shaped arrangement of cell blocks. But when actually built (between 1959 and 1962), Grendon's cell blocks had floors rather than open corridors, and the Y-plan wing was replaced by a pair of wings flanking the main corridor.

Although open landings were abandoned at Grendon, they were employed at two other contemporary prisons, in 'A' Wing at HMP Hull (1958–60), and the small female borstal, now HMP & YOI Bullwood Hall (1959–62).

While these prisons were in progress, a series of fundamental changes occurred as a direct result of vociferous criticism which Everthorpe attracted. A 'Development Group for the Design of Prisons' was established in September 1958 to improve the design and security of prisons and to reduce their cost. By June 1959 they had produced a scheme for a new type of prison in which four T-plan wings were arranged around a central service block (see page 30).

The wings were to be four-storied and each spur was four bays long. The ground floor was to be used for association, dining and offices, while the three upper floors were occupied by small cells and dormitories. WCs were not included in cells as inmates would be outside the cells for most of the day. Dining rooms were provided since eating in the smaller cells would be impractical. The central service block contained classrooms, a library, the canteen and gym on the ground floor, and the first floor housed the four dining rooms and kitchen. The Anglican and Roman Catholic chapels were on the top floor.

HMP Blundeston opened in July 1963 and was the first of the so-called 'New Wave' prisons which were to be

HMP Everthorpe. Interior of wing with cells opening from landings flanking an open, top-lit corridor (1956–8).

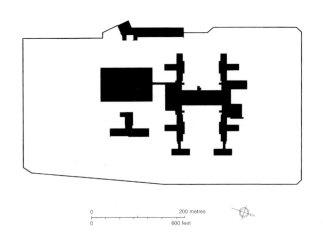

above: General view of wing,
HMP Grendon, Buckinghamshire
(1959–62). Open landings were
abandoned at Grendon.

right: Block plan HMP
Blundeston, Suffolk (1961–3).
The first of the 'New Wave'
prisons, with four T-plan wings.

0   200 metres
0   600 feet

HMP Stoke Heath, Shrewsbury. General view of wing and central service block of the 'New Wave' prison (1961–4).

the dominant architectural form of the 1960s. However, some of the new forms had already been anticipated at HMP Hindley which opened in December 1961. A sensational head-line in *The Times* on 7 December 1961 described it as a 'Public School for Young Offenders', with 'TV sets to Hire'! Its plan consisted of four T-plan wings, similar in form to the wings at Blundeston — arranged around a complex of buildings comparable to those at Everthorpe.

Blundeston offered a new vision of training and treatment for inmates and its buildings were to reflect this.

It marked the start of a huge construction programme which, mirroring the spirit of the times, was expected to dramatically improve the state of England's prisons and ultimately replace all the despised Victorian local prisons.

However, seventeen new purpose-built prisons were conceived in the 1960s, but no Victorian prisons closed. The optimism of the early 1960s was to be defeated by the inexorable rise of the prison popula-tion, and was undermined by the shortcomings which became evident within the new prisons themselves.

Prisons in the 1970s and 1980s — the Pressure for Places

New Wave prisons established standard plans based on floored wings with small cells located on short spurs, and this type of wing design became the basis of most prisons until the late 1980s. The growing prison population in the 1970s and 1980s required larger prisons. The compact centralised plan of Blundeston could not be enlarged to achieve this and therefore a new expanded plan form was developed.

The earliest example is Featherstone, begun in 1973, and open to receive the first of its 484 inmates in November 1976 (see page 35). Prisoners are accommodated in two separate houseblocks, each consisting of four pairs of perpendicular short spurs with adjacent dining and association areas. Every element of the prison — except the huge work-shop complex — is linked by corridors. This type of houseblock continued to be used in the early 1980s, and a slightly modified version was used at Brinsford, which opened as late as 1991. The 1970s also saw the use of a linear plan at Acklington where three wings were attached to a linking corridor block and at Kirklevington Grange where a similar layout was created adjacent to the country house.

A houseblock in one of the large new prisons was capable of accommodating between 200 and 250 prisoners, allowing a prison such as Wymott to house 816 prisoners in wings similar to Featherstone. An alternative approach was to create a campus layout with a series of smaller houseblocks which could be connected by a complex of corridors. At Castington, Deerbolt and at Stocken, the houseblocks consist of a pair of perpendicular floored spurs containing the cells, attached to a block containing dining areas, association rooms and offices.

Although the plans of prisons of the 1970s and 1980s have clear links to their New Wave predecessors, there was a profound change in architectural style. In the 1960s the wings were relatively tall and narrow with pitched roofs with broad eaves. The windows with their simplified glazing pattern and the security ironwork employing squares add to the distinctive character of the wings. The central service blocks placed great emphasis on the triangular section of their roofs in which the chapels were accommodated and created a line of concrete flying buttresses. The glass brick was raised from the pavement to serve as the decorative backdrop for waiting rooms, corridors and even a chapel.

The penal architecture of the 1970s and 1980s was very different. Houseblocks were lower, wider and plainer. Through the use of flat roofs they became very cubic in form. In a prison such as Featherstone the only articulation on the exterior of the wings is provided by the cell windows, though this scarcely relieves the monotony of the walls. Some architects seem to have been conscious of the severity of the blocks and exploited the few architectural features which were available to them. Pier and panel construction was employed at some prisons, a practical construction technique which also served to improve the exterior appearance. In other prisons the cell windows are treated as a continuous glazed band running around the whole wing.

left: Detail of wing (1961–4), HMYOI Stoke Heath, Shropshire. Distinctive New Wave detailing in the geometrical window ironwork.

below: HMP Grendon, Buckinghamshire. Interior of chapel (1959–62).

HMYOI Deerbolt, County
Durham. General view of
houseblock (1973–86), with later
alterations to original flat roofs.

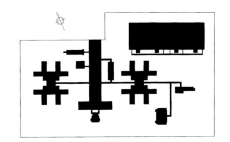

above: HMP Featherstone, Staffordshire. General view of houseblock (1973–6). The influence of the 1960s New Wave prisons persists in the layout of the wings.

left: HMP Featherstone, Staffordshire. Block plan.

left: The 1970s: HMP The Verne, Dorset. General view of wing (1972–5).

right: General view, HMP Holloway, London (1970–83). Holloway was conceived as a secure hospital for 500 women.

below: City House of Correction Holloway, London. James Bunstone Bunning (1849–52). General view of the Victorian prison, replaced in the 1970s and 80s.

The rebuilding of Holloway

The largest construction project of the 1970s was the only example of fulfilling the dream of replacing a Victorian prison — with a new purpose-built facility. Proposals to rebuild the City House of Correction at Holloway had been made in the 1930s, but it was not until the 1970s that the project was finally begun. The demolition and building work was phased to enable the prison to remain operational. Work began in October 1970 and was due to be completed in 1977 at an estimated cost of £6 million. However, delays meant that it was not finally finished until 1983.

Holloway was conceived as a secure hospital for 500 women. The living accommodation was deliberately sited away from the work, education and recreational facilities, to preserve the concept of 'going out' to work.

The new prison was to provide therapeutic medical and psychiatric treatment for the patients, who were to be housed according to the type of treatment they required. By the 1980s the emphasis moved to the provision of training, although Holloway still provides accommodation for prisoners requiring specialist medical treatment. Pregnant women are housed in a maternity unit and there is a separate mother and baby unit (see also HMP Askham Grange, North Yorkshire, pages 67 and 96).

above: HMYOI & RC Feltham, London. General view of a houseblock (1975–88).

right: Block plan, HMYOI & RC Feltham, London (1975–88).

opposite: HMYOI & RC Feltham, London. Interior of houseblock (1975–88).

0   200 metres

0   600 feet

A 'New Generation' of Prisons

By the end of the 1970s there was a recognition of the limitations of the new designs and a realisation that new approaches should be examined. In 1975 it was decided that a new borstal should be built at Feltham. The borstal, which opened in August 1983, shares common facilities with the remand centre which was completed in March 1988. The new borstal buildings are the first examples in England of the adoption of ideas from 'New Generation' American prisons. They are arranged in an informal campus-type layout and are linked by a 'business street'. The scale and irregularity of the individual blocks, as well as the trees and grassed areas, disguise the penal nature of the institution. Each of the units at Feltham holds thirty-two trainees in two-storied triangular houseblocks, with the cells arranged around an association area. The detailing of the blocks is deliberately non-industrial, and the direct lighting from the main window creates an open, light atmosphere in the blocks. Similar units were built at Erlestoke and at Guys Marsh during the 1980s.

Larger triangular houseblocks were the basis for the new prisons at Lancaster Farms, Woodhill and Doncaster which opened in the early 1990s. At Doncaster one houseblock is placed above another, resulting in the lower one having limited natural lighting. However, at Woodhill the reverse is achieved. By placing the cells on two sides of the unit, the third side could be devoted to a single vast window which allows light to stream into the association area.

Introducing light and air was achieved in other ways in a series of prisons built in the late 1980s and 1990s. Two cell blocks which opened at HMP Standford Hill in 1986 were the first wings since the early 1960s to employ open landings with cells opening from galleries. These wings led to an immediate change in the design of new prisons. Although the plans continued to be related to designs of the 1960s, with cruciform wings linked to a centralised complex of facilities, the internal appearance of the wings was transformed. The new prisons Belmarsh, Whitemoor and Bullingdon (opened in 1991 and 1992), were the first of this new type of prison. The wings were linked to each other and to their central services by two-storied corridors. Inmates could be moved along the secure upper corridor while the open ground floor corridor could be used by staff and as the route for food trolleys. As accommodation was required urgently, the decision was taken to build five further prisons based on the Bullingdon plan, including HMP Holme House, Cleveland.

left: HMP Doncaster, South Yorkshire, interior of cell block. Opened 1994.

above: General view of chapel and walkways at the centre of the prison, HMP Holme House, Cleveland (opened 1992). One of five prisons modelled on Bullingdon.

HMP Woodhill, Buckinghamshire
(opened 1993). Interior of
houseblock — a single vast
window allows light to stream
into the association area.

HMP Bullingdon, Oxfordshire
(opened 1992). Wing interior.

Refurbishing and Improving Prisons

The other major development around 1990 was a major refurbishment programme of older prisons. Disturbances at forty-six prisons in 1986 led to the start of this programme, but it was the public spectacle of inmates on the roof of HMP Manchester for twenty-five days in April 1990 which accelerated it. Wings were refurbished to improve the facilities and security. They were subdivided so that prisoners would in the future be held in units of around fifty to sixty cells. In-cell sanitation was again installed allowing all prisoners access to sanitation at night.

Since the late 1980s the Prison Service has been under growing pressure to supply sufficient accommodation for a rapidly rising prison population. This has led the development of standard plans for kitchens, sports halls and wings. The earliest of these standard wings, the so-called 'Bedford Unit', is rectangular in plan with cells on three sides and offices and facilities on the other. Other standard blocks resemble Victorian wings, with cells opening from landings.

top: HMP Manchester, Greater Manchester. Interior of refurbished wing (1990–3).

bottom: HMP Hindley, Greater Manchester. Interior of new standard unit wing (DOW II; opened 1996).

right: HMYOI Onley, Warwickshire. Bedford Unit interior (DOW I; 1988/9–1990/1).

The Emergency Accommodation Programme

The prison population began to rise more rapidly in 1996 and 1997 prompting an emergency accommodation programme. A standard pre-fabricated design of houseblock (DOW VI) was developed with a pair of two-storey wings flanking a central area containing offices and other facilities. They are constructed using modules which are delivered on the backs of lorries and by the end of the decade they will have provided 3,000 extra places.

The Prison Service is also providing additional places in Ready to Use Units (RTUs; see page 48). These were originally designed for oil workers accommodation in Norway, but with some modifications have proved suitable for use in low security prisons.

The most publicised emergency measure for dealing with the rising population was the opening of HMP

left: General view of new wing (DOW VI; completed summer 1997) HMYOI Wetherby, North Yorkshire.

above: HMP Garth, Lancashire. Interior of new wing (DOW VI; completed spring 1997).

Weare. Originally known as 'Bibby Resolution', it was one of two barges constructed by Bibby Freighters Ltd of Liverpool as a barracks for troops after the United Kingdom recaptured the Falkland Islands. In 1987 it was towed to New York where it served as a prison and in 1997 was moved to Portland Harbour. Weare is capable of holding 400 inmates accommodated in a five-storey block. It contains most of the facilities required by the prisoners, including the kitchen, gymnasium and chapel.

letf: HMP Send, Surrey. General view of Ready to Use unit (built spring 1997).

above: General view of prison, HMP Weare, Dorset.

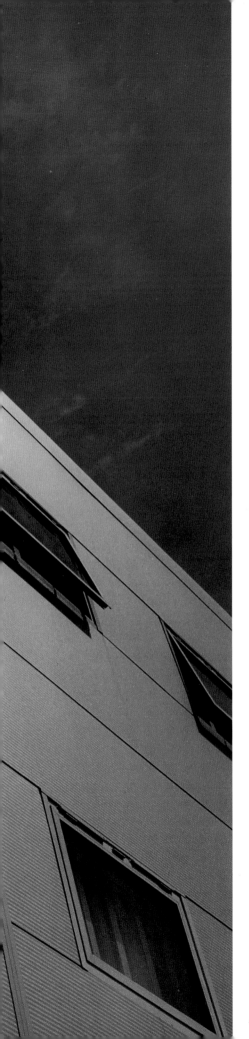

Private Prisons

Since 1992, private companies have managed prisons and these form a small but increasing proportion of the prison estate. HMP Wolds was built by the Property Services Agency (PSA) for the Prison Service but when it opened as the Wolds Remand Prison in April 1992 its management was contracted to Group 4. Two other PSA-built prisons at Doncaster and Buckley Hall have contracted-out management, but more recently the private sector has become responsible for the design, construction, management and financing (DCMF) of new prisons. The first three have opened at Altcourse, Parc and Lowdham Grange, and contracts for four other DCMF prisons have recently been agreed. These most recent prisons owe a clear debt to designs produced for the Prison Service since the late 1980s but they also reveal ideas imported from the USA, this time because of the close business connections of the security firms which manage them.

left: HMP Parc, Mid Glamorgan, detail of cell block. Opened at the end of 1997.

above: HMP Parc, Mid Glamorgan. General view of cell block (opened at the end of 1997).

Behind Bars
The Prison Buildings

The Gate

The gate marks the transition between the world outside and the world inside prison. It is usually the only part of the prison that the public sees and is designed with this in mind. It is also designed to be reassuringly secure, and in the 18th and early 19th centuries consciously resembled a robust classical monument or a castle. By the end of the 19th century, gates were more utilitarian and austere, a reflection of the sober conditions to be found within. When faced with the prospect of designing a secure prison in the 1950s, the architects recreated the simple form of seventy years earlier but used contemporary materials and forms.

The gate is the point of access to a prison, but also contains a key room and, in early prisons, some basic reception facilities. A small prison like Littledean in the 1780s (see page 7) had a fumigating room and baths adjacent to the gate. During the 19th century and up to 1960, the gate was usually simply an entrance, but during the 1960s its function and appearance were redefined. It was then to contain the administration and visits room and was therefore consciously designed to resemble an office block rather than a fortress. In the past thirty years the gate has continued to perform this wider range of functions, though the architectural style has returned to more robust forms.

above left: General view of gate, HMP Wormwood Scrubs, London. Edmund Du Cane (1874–91). Probably the most famous prison gate in England, the two plaques commemorate the work of Elizabeth Fry and John Howard.

above right: General view of gate, HMP & RC Exeter, Devon. George Moneypenny (1807–9) and John Hayward (1853). The gate was part of the house of correction which was amalgamated with the county gaol in 1853, when Hayward added two-storied houses for the chaplain and governor on either side of the gate.

right: HMP Leicester, Leicestershire. General view of gate, built in the style of a medieval castle, William Parsons (1825–8). In addition to serving as the entrance to the prison, it also contained punishment cells for inmates who infringed rules.

HMYOI Stoke Heath,
Shropshire. General view of gate
(1961–4). In the New Wave
prisons of the 1960s,
pedestrians enter the prison
through an entry building
reminiscent of an office block,
while vehicles enter through a
separate gate.

above right: HMP Hindley, Greater Manchester. General view of gate (1959–61). Like Wormwood Scrubs, this gate is simply an entrance into the prison. The starkness of its architecture reflects the tradition of the utilitarian gates of Prison Commissioners' prisons at the end of the 19th century.

above left: General view of gate (late 1980s), HMP Birmingham, West Midlands. This huge complex replaced a Victorian gate which was too small for modern transport. Like 1960s gates, it has separate entries for pedestrians and vehicles, and contains the visits room, administration and reception. The central motif of the gate echoes the turrets of the structure which it replaced.

HMP Lowdham Grange,
Nottinghamshire. Inmate and
officer completing registration
papers. The arrival of new
inmates from court or from
another prison involves the
compilation of new records.
Written records are drawn up
and photographs taken for both
records and identification cards.

Reception

On arriving at prison, every inmate's first experience is the reception unit. Registration records are compiled which include fingerprints and photographs, and records from any previous prison must also be incorporated. Registers of prisoners survive from the beginning of the 19th century — including by the middle of that century, photographs. Property which is not appropriate for use inside the prison has to be stored in the reception, sometimes for years. In a local prison dealing with large numbers of prisoners travelling to and from court, the reception unit may deal with hundreds of receptions and discharges each year.

After being received at a local prison new inmates serving a longer prison sentence are placed on an induction wing to assess the type of prison to which they should be sent to serve their sentence. At training prisons (for sentenced inmates only), new arrivals may take part in induction classes which explain the rules and regulations and describe the facilities which are available. In an open prison this can be particularly important as inmates may be experiencing an environment where they have a large amount of personal responsibility after years of following a strict routine in a secure prison.

19th-century photographs of inmates. Photography was introduced into prisons in the third quarter of the 19th century. Inmates posed with their hands on their chest so that any injury or amputation could be recorded. Source: Prison Service Museum, Newbold Revel, Warwickshire.

left: Property room, HMP Wandsworth, Greater London. A large prison requires a large property room, and a local prison with a rapid turnover of inmates sees property being deposited and withdrawn daily.

above: Induction class, HMP Spring Hill, Buckinghamshire. On starting a prison sentence or on arriving at a new prison, inmates may take part in induction classes. This can be particularly important in an open prison, as inmates may be experiencing an environment where they have a large amount of personal responsibility after years following the strict routine of a secure prison.

Cells, Dormitories and Cubicles

At the heart of the prison experience is the cell, dormitory or cubicle. The cell, an invention of the 18th century, was inspired by medieval monastic precedents. Like its religious predecessors it was to be a place of contemplation, allowing the offender time to reflect on their crime. Originally for occupation during the night only, the introduction of the separate system in the 1840s meant that inmates spent twenty-three hours a day in their cells. Prisoners ate, washed, worked and slept in them. A simple toilet and washbasin were incorporated in Victorian cells to allow this, but these were removed by the end of the 19th century, as they were prone to blockages and leaks.

Before cells were provided, most prisoners slept communally in large rooms. Dormitories were replaced during the 19th century but with the creation of borstals in hutted settlements they assumed a new importance. Today some open and Category C prisons, both in former military camps and in country houses, provide dormitory accommodation for short-term imprisonment. Some dormitories are subdivided into small cubicles to provide an element of privacy.

The cell has changed dramatically during the course of the present century. The severe austerity of the late 19th century cell, devoid of any human expression, has gradually evolved into a more homely environment in which basic creature comforts are provided. Although all cells are approximately the same size, each occupant finds ways of customising his or her own living space.

above: Cell, Newgate Gaol, Greater London (1857–9). Late 19th century photograph. The standard Victorian cell originally contained a hammock — replaced after 1865 by the plank bed. The toilet and wash basin in the corner meant that inmates could be held in their cells for up to twenty-three hours a day.

right: Cell interior, HMP Usk, Gwent. For thousands of inmates the Victorian cell still serves as their home. Cell toilets and washbasins were mostly removed by the end of the 19th century, but since 1990 have again been installed.

above left: Cell interior, HMP
Hull, Kingston upon Hull.

above right: Cell interior, HMP
The Wolds, East Yorkshire.

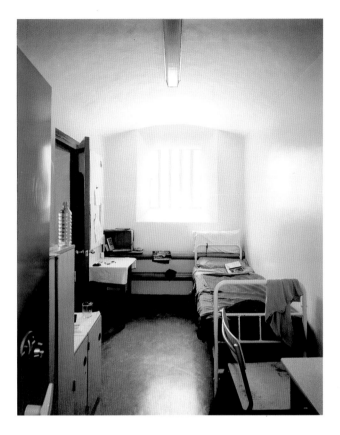

above left: Cell interior, HMP
Norwich, Norfolk.

above right: Cell interior, HMP
Liverpool, Merseyside.

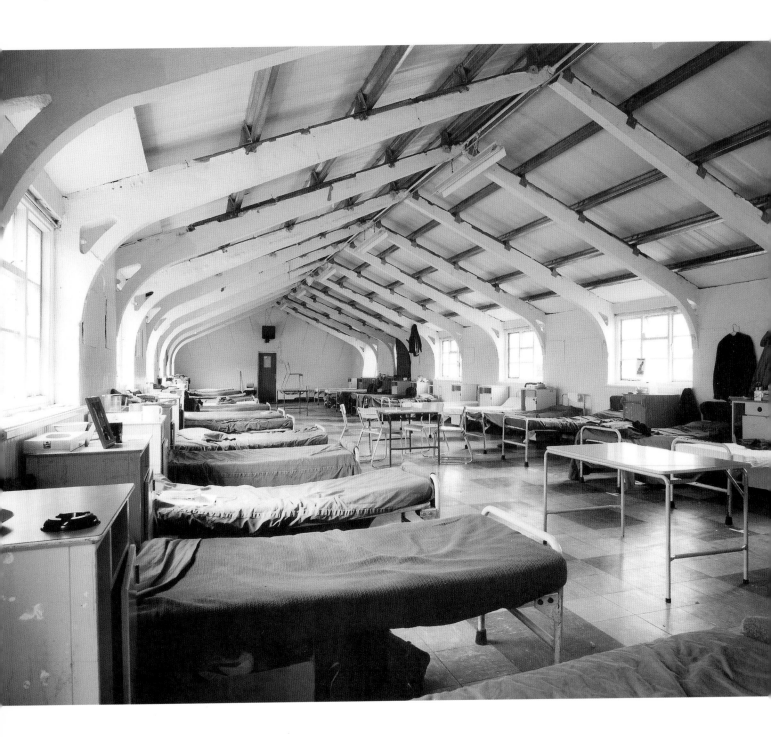

left: Interior of dormitory, HMP Sudbury, Derbyshire (1942). Many of the former US Army Hospital huts are used as dormitories at this open prison, while others contain recreation facilities and other amenities.

above: Bedroom in Mother and Baby Unit, HMP Askham Grange, North Yorkshire. Four prisons have these units which allow children to stay with their mother until they are eighteen months old.

Double cell interior, HMYOI
Lancaster Farms, Lancashire.
Some prisons have purpose-built
double cells which have an
adjacent area containing the
toilet and basin and an additional
sitting area.

Double cell interior, HMP
Blakenhurst, Worcestershire. An
alternative approach to double
occupancy of the cell.

Punishment cell in gate, HMP
Leicester, Leicestershire. William
Parsons (1825–8). Prisoners who
infringed rules in the prison were
sent to small, dark, cold cells in
the upper storey of the gate.

Segregation Unit

Throughout history prisons have had some inmates who proved difficult to control. Misbehaviour could lead to corporal punishment — an option which was only removed from the statute book in 1967. At Newgate there was a whipping block which survives today in the Prison Service Museum.

In addition to physical punishment, prisoners who broke rules could be sent to 'refractory cells' which were often in the basements of wings. They were dark, cold and largely unfurnished, and the occupants were subject to a poorer diet than in the rest of the prison.

Today, almost every prison has a segregation unit. The unit contains cells where inmates are consigned when they first present control problems. They are deliberately devoid of anything which could be used either for self-harm or as a weapon. Most of the segregation unit is made up of very austere cells where inmates are expected to spend short periods before returning to their wings or being moved to another prison. Exercise is limited to short periods in a yard which is both secure and barren. It is hoped that a short stay in the unit and the loss of some privileges or remission will engender an improvement in behaviour.

Interior of segregation unit, HMP Hindley, Greater Manchester (1959–61). The segregation unit is the starkest part of the prison. Apart from the cells the only other element is a small servery for the food and a staff office.

71

above: Segregation unit yard, HMP Hindley, Greater Manchester (1959–61). Segregation units have small exercise yards adjacent to the wing which inmates can only use alone.

right: Interior of segregation unit cell, HMP Hindley, Greater Manchester (1959–61). Inmates are punished by being held in these cells with no privileges. The furniture is made of strong cardboard and the bed is fixed to the floor.

Chapel

Today, every prison has a chapel but when John Howard first travelled around English prisons in the 1770s they were rare. Howard advocated that every prison should have a chapel and that there should be a salaried chaplain to minister to the inmates. Religion was to be part of the process of reform and throughout the 19th century it played a central role in imprisonment. The separate system required the inmate attending a religious service to be able to see the preacher but prevented him from communicating with other inmates.

Today, religion plays an important part in the life of the prison community, and the chapel is often the one place within prisons which is indistinguishable from its equivalent on the outside. Many prisons also cater for inmates of non-Christian faiths. In smaller prisons a multi-faith room can be adapted for use by a range of religions, but in some larger prisons dedicated mosques and temples are created.

above left: Exterior of chapel, HMP Channings Wood, Devon (late 1970s). The chapel is usually physically as well as spiritually at the centre of the prison and, like the gate, is often designed as an architectural statement.

above right: Interior of chapel, HMP Lincoln, Lincolnshire. Frederick Peck (1869–72 and later refurbishment). Modern chapels in large prisons are now used for all Christian denominations and can also serve as a community hall.

Interior of chapel, HMP
Wormwood Scrubs, London.
Edmund Du Cane (1874–91).
This is the largest chapel in the
prison system, capable of
holding over 1000 worshippers.

Healthcare

John Howard was concerned with the physical as well as spiritual welfare of prisoners. One of his first achievements was to obtain an Act of Parliament in 1774 which required separate rooms to be provided for sick prisoners and the appointment of an experienced surgeon or apothecary. Infirmaries in early prisons were often in the governor's house, but by the mid 19th-century the male infirmary was usually in the administration block or adjacent to the male wings, while the female one was located beside the female wing. At the end of the 19th century, the size and scope of hospitals increased and new blocks which also contained reception facilities were built. Since the 1960s separate hospitals have been provided.

Healthcare is an important feature of the modern Prison Service. Major surgery and other complicated medical procedures are undertaken in outside hospitals, but in prison a wide range of medical care is provided. In addition to prison healthcare staff, local doctors, dentists and some specialists hold clinics in prisons. Prison healthcare staff are also involved in preventive medicine campaigns, particularly in the areas of drug awareness and HIV prevention.

above left: HMP & YOI Moorland, South Yorkshire. An optician regularly visits the prison to test inmate's eyes.

above right: Dental treatment at HMP Buckley Hall, Lancashire. Dentists also hold clinics in prisons, both to provide regular check ups and to deal with particular problems.

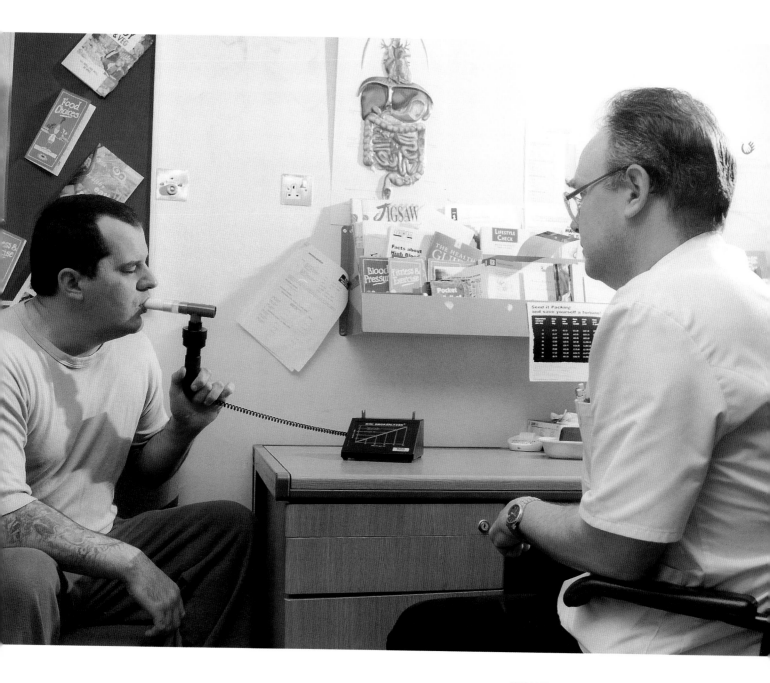

HMP & YOI Moorland, South Yorkshire. Preventive medicine. Prison health-care staff are involved in educating prisoners about health issues, including explaining the dangers of smoking, one of their most common recreations.

The Workplace

For convicted prisoners a large part of the day in prison is spent at work. In the 19th century this was usually unproductive punitive labour on the treadwheel or involved sewing, weaving or cobbling in the cells. In the 1890s the use of the treadwheel ceased and productive industrial workshops were created, often in the former treadwheel sheds. During both Wars, prisons were active in providing war materials and the notorious sewing of mailbags was a common sight in prisons in the first half of this century.

Today the Prison Service has a wide variety of workshops, producing goods for outside contractors, government departments and for other parts of the Prison Service. Many of the laundries carry out work for local hospitals and some of the craft workshops produce items to raise money for charity. At some of the larger prisons extensive farming is undertaken, producing a wide range of foodstuffs for sale and for use elsewhere in the prison system.

left: Textiles workshop, HMP Bristol, Bristol and South Gloucestershire. Many prisons have large textiles workshops, where a wide variety of products are prepared for use elsewhere in the Prison Service and for private contracts. As well as providing employment, the training they offer can prove helpful in gaining employment on release.

above: Late 19th-century photograph of men on the treadwheel at HMP Kingston, Portsmouth, Hampshire. From its invention in 1818 until its abolition at the end of the 19th century, thousands of inmates spent up to eight hours a day on the treadwheel. Some of these powered corn mills or water pumps, but many others were purely punitive, driving no machinery.

Cows coming in for milking, farm at HMP Rochester, Kent. Many rural prisons have large farms which produce vegetables, meat and dairy products for use in the Prison Service. Rochester produces small cartons of milk for use in local prisons, while the dairy farm at nearby HMP & YOI East Sutton Park produces Mozzarella for a private company.

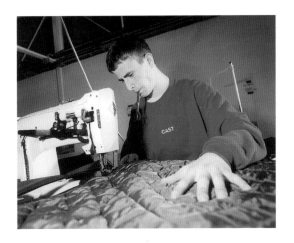 

above left: Inmate sewing,
HMYOI Castington,
Northumberland.

above right: Inmate welding,
HMP Dartmoor, Devon.

Training and Education

Work within the prison system is designed to occupy an inmate's time productively. However, it also seeks to provide some real work experience and practical training which could help the prisoner find employment on release. Training courses in building skills, decorating and car mechanics are widely available and some prisons also offer opportunities to learn computing, catering and hairdressing.

In addition to training, each prison offers educational opportunities, ranging from basic literacy to degree courses through the Open University. Education departments are faced with the problem of encouraging pupils who have not succeeded in their earlier schooling, and with difficulties created by the rapid turnover of inmates in prison, making preparation for examinations difficult. Inspite of these difficulties, many prisons have successful records of achievement in vocational and academic qualifications.

Each year there is a competition to recognise the best examples of art, pottery, needlecraft, model-making, woodwork, photography, creative writing and music. The Koestler Awards Scheme, originally established by the late Arthur Koestler, receives more than 2,000 entries annually from almost every prison, young offender institution and special hospital in the country.

above: Prisoner in art class, HMP Featherstone, Staffordshire.

right: The art classroom, HMP Wormwood Scrubs, London. Every prison has an education department offering a wide range of courses, some of which lead to academic and vocational qualifications. Art is a particularly popular subject and many inmates take advantage of the opportunity to discover new talents for the first time.

above left: Motor mechanics at HMP & YOI Moorland, South Yorkshire. Modern prisons offer a wide range of practical training courses designed to help prisoners find work on release. These include building skills, car maintenance, industrial cleaning and hairdressing.

above right: Training in industrial cleaning. HMYOI Deerbolt, County Durham.

right: Hairdressing class at HMP Downview, Surrey.

Kitchen and Dining Facilities

One of the most important tasks within a prison is catering for the inmates. A catering officer is provided with just £1.50 per day to feed each inmate on a diet that is both nutritious and varied. A further complication is that special diets have to be provided for people with special requirements (vegetarians, vegans, Muslims, Jews, diabetics and those requiring a low-fat diet, etc.). The kitchen is a hive of activity during the morning and afternoon until it is time for the trolleys to be loaded which deliver the food to each wing. When each meal is completed the duty governor tastes the food to ensure that it meets prison standards.

Under the 'separate system', prisoners ate alone in their cells, but during the 20th century they have been allowed to dine communally, either on the ground floor of wings or in purpose-built dining areas. However, owing to security concerns, communal dining rooms at some prisons have now been converted into association areas.

top: The kitchen, HMYOI & RC Feltham, London. Prisons have large kitchens capable of catering for hundreds of inmates; they also provide work and work-experience for a number of the inmates.

bottom: Prisoners cooking in HMP Kirkham, Lancashire.

The kitchen at HMP Ford, West Sussex.

Visiting Rooms

Until late in the 18th century, visitors were allowed relatively free access to prisons. On payment of a fee, they could visit a relative or see celebrity prisoners such as Jacobites or notorious highwaymen. The ease of visiting undoubtedly contributed to the air of disorder within early prisons.

By the 19th century, however, visiting had been restricted to short, occasional visits by immediate relatives who were only permitted to see their imprisoned loved one through a grill. In the early 1920s these visiting boxes were abolished. Instead, inmates and their families could now face each other across a table. The format for most visits is the same today. However, where a prisoner or their visitors have infringed visiting regulations, they may only receive a closed visit in a booth where no physical contact is permitted.

Since 1990 prisons have been creating visitors centres which lie outside the prison and provide a place for visitors to congregate before entering the prison. These new facilities also contain lockers for personal property and refreshment facilities for waiting visitors.

top left: A visit, HMP & YOI Moorland, South Yorkshire.

top right: HMP Belmarsh, Woolwich, Greater London. The creation of Visitors Centres was recommended in 1990 as a measure to improve the experience of visiting an inmate.

right: Interior of visits block, HMP Hindley, Greater Manchester (1996). Instead of a grilled visiting cubicle, most visits since the 1920s have been conducted around tables, in large visits halls.

Behind Bars
People in Prison

Staff

Until the late 18th century, prison staff had to rely on fees paid by inmates. The creation of salaried staff was one of the first of John Howard's reforms. The status of prison work gradually rose during the 19th century, and this was reflected in staff housing.

Under the separate system the whole prison was managed in silence with staff wearing felt overshoes so that their footsteps would not be heard. In the 19th century, staff had little personal contact with prisoners, but by the 1920s a limited amount of conversation was permitted. In 1922 warders were renamed 'officers' to reflect their changing role and the greater involvement they were to have with the rehabilitation and training of prisoners.

Today, prison officers and the civilian staff who work in prison are involved in the running of a complex institution housing hundreds of prisoners carrying out a broad range of activities. They are also responsible for the day-to-day administration of the prison and for enforcing prison regulations.

Specialist staff carry out security checks and searches, sometimes supported by teams of trained dogs.

opposite: Controlling access to the prison, HMP & YOI Moorland, South Yorkshire.

top: Staff opening the post, to ensure that nothing inappropriate is sent into the prison, HMP Cookham Wood, Kent.

middle: Officers using drug-testing equipment, HMP Holme House, Cleveland. Urine tests have been introduced in prisons in an attempt to prevent the misuse of drugs.

bottom: Dog searching for drugs in a cell in HMP & YOI Moorland, South Yorkshire. Trained dogs can detect where drugs were previously located.

Inmates

Until the late 18th century, inmates who could pay the required fees had access to any food, drink or sexual pleasures which they could afford. Poor inmates had to rely on charity to pay for food. Reforms in the late 18th century led to men, women, juveniles and debtors being held separately, and during the early 19th century these groups were further subdivided according to the gravity of their crime.

The separate system meant that every inmate was held in his or her own cell and they were forbidden to speak at any time, a regime which regularly led to madness. Chapels were designed

above left: Inmates walking around exercise rings in the 1970s, HMP Winchester, Hampshire. Although no longer compelled to march around the rings, as in the 19th century, inmates still continued to use them for exercise. Most rings have now been replaced by plain yards or gardens.

above right: Football match, HMP Gartree, Leicestershire. Weather permitting, the exercise periods are usually a time for a football match.

right: Darts game, HMP & YOI Moorland, South Yorkshire. At Moorland a branch of the YMCA has been opened in a wing where inmates, staff and volunteers can meet, relax and talk. It also helps prisoners to find jobs and accommodation in preparation for their release.

to prevent inmates communicating and this isolation was even extended to exercise periods where inmates either had individual yards or wore masks and walked in line. Individual yards were replaced with exercise rings which have now mostly been replaced by plain yards or gardens.

In the late 19th century, inmates were allowed to work in groups and in the 1920s the absolute rule of silence was relaxed. The last vestiges of the separate system finally disappeared in the late 1950s when it was recognised that staff and inmates would both benefit by more human contact. Today a wide range of recreational opportunities are available in prisons during association periods. At some prisons very specialised and ambitious activities have been developed by interested staff and inmates.

above left: Jim and Bert, HMP Featherstone, Staffordshire. Jim and an officer have established a sanctuary for rescued birds of prey. They also hatch eggs seized from collectors by the police and rear the birds. Bert is a European eagle owl.

above right: Lunchtime, HMP Askham Grange, North Yorkshire. During lunch hour the women prisoners spend time with their children before returning to work in the afternoon.

Tony feeding his budgerigar,
HMP Grendon, Buckinghamshire.
At some prisons inmates are
allowed to keep small birds in
their cells.